Rimfire

Rimfire

Romaine Moreton
Alf Taylor
Michael J. Smith

Magabala Books

First published in 2000 by Magabala Books Aboriginal Corporation, 2/28 Saville Street, PO Box 668, Broome, Western Australia 6725
Email: magabala@tpgi.com.au

Magabala Books receives financial assistance from the Commonwealth Government through the Australia Council, its arts funding and advisory body, and the Aboriginal and Torres Strait Islander Commission. The State of Western Australia has made an investment in this project through ArtsWA in association with the Lotteries Commission.

Printed by Australian Print Group
Typeset in New Baskerville11/12.5pt
National Library of Australia
Cataloguing-in-Publication data:

Moreton, Romaine
Rimfire

ISBN 1 875641 59 9

1. Aborigines, Australian - Poetry. 2. Australian poetry - Aboriginal authors. I. Taylor, Alf, 1947- . II. Smith, Michael J., 1964- . III, Singer Songwriter. IV. Title.

A821.308089915

Contents

The Callused Stick of Wanting

Romaine Moreton

Romaine Moreton is a performance poet and writer. Romaine has been writing poetry for ten years, and has been doing public performances of her work for about five years, her most recent performances including appearances at the Sydney Opera House. Romaine is also a writer for film, two of her films having been sent to fringe festivals in Cannes. *Cherish*, written in 1997, was included in a package of student works from all over the country, while *Redreaming The Dark* also appeared in film festivals in Cannes and New York. Romaine has a B.A. in Communications, and an M.A. in Screenwriting.

Photo courtesy of Vanessa Mason.

Author's Note

The Callused Stick of Wanting was written with the intention of poetry becoming a site of resistance. Initial rejection letters from publishers stated that the collection of poetry presented to them was more polemic than poetic. With this in mind, the author intentionally focuses on the originality of the myriad of black voices that exist in this country, and states them as her inspiration.

This collection of poetry was written over a three year period, and was privately published during 1996. *The Callused Stick of Wanting* is being used in various universities around the country, and has also been used internationally as a resource—for example, in Santa Cruz University's Women's Studies curriculum. Various works from the collection will be performed during a half hour documentary on the author's work at the end of 2000, (on-air date to be confirmed) as part of the Indigenous film maker's initiative. Romaine has performed works from this collection at various cultural festivals.

Contents

This book is dedicated to the memory of Aunt Ellen, and to all my Mothers, Desley, Beryl, Rose, Hazel and May.

Time for Dreaming

Where the shadows fall as the sun rises,
that is your Dreaming.
When the early morning skies erupt into a collage
of inner soul pink,
and the mountains vie for your attention,
it is time for you
to go.

Do not wonder about the ways of the whiteman
for they have already run their course,
do not worry about the debts of the whiteman
for you have already fully paid.

This is your redemption
and it is the only time you have
for time is fast approaching
its end.

Sanguine

Life has become a precious thing,
and I worship the moments
that allow me
to be,
whether appreciating friendship
or shedding tears
over what was,
or what will probably never be.

Do not hold tightly onto that which can be purged by fire
and water,
but rather that which you can hold only
in spirit and thought,
emotion and memory.

I have come to respect
mortality
and the finiteness of time

That what is now
is not
Forever

Each moment passes
into the next

And one day
your regrets
may multiply,
because while you were regretting
you were forgetting
that
Life is short.

The first sin

He was guilty of the first sin—
Being black

He was sentenced very early in life—
At birth

and only substances appeased his pangs of guilt.

There he sat,
his rostrum, the dock

being viewed by his peers,
his overseers

as they waited to condemn.

His mother too
was guilty,

all prejudice being a variation of the same.

She,
the Mary,

who bore society a child
ready for the crucifix

to save their souls,
appease their anger.

She readied herself to leave,
but feared that she would bow and scrape incorrectly

to the Great White Hopelessness
in a wig.

Instead,
wiggles uncomfortably in her seat.

He rubs the back of his leg,
where
crushing black baton
and crushing black bones

became one.

His sentence,
his dilemma,
is   another stripe
          another day
          another drink of commemoration
          another joke

to these argent agents,
For All are Seduced
                Convinced
by the hoar whore
named
Justice.

Mr Slave Mentality

Ten Times Out of Nine,
I have the misfortune of meeting Mr Slave Mentality.

His mind,
the smell of baby vomit that hasn't been cleaned for a week,
thrusts dirty dollar bills in my direction.

'Brown Sugar Brown Sugar
Be my Brown Sugar!'
as he looked at me,
eyes
the windows of hell that have never been washed,
searching for response,
finding none.

I have the choice now
to say No!
and I say
No!
But Mr Slave Mentality
wants his brown sugar,
can't drink his whisky without it,
and as he takes a step closer
I can smell his breath,
volcanic ash spewing forth.

I am not flattered
or care
for his filthy fifty dollar bills
because money bought the slaves
that cut the sugar cane field,
and money killed the black men and women
who sweeten a nation's tea,

but money won't buy a little brown sugar
like me.

He puts his hand to his chest,
mock despair,
over
his heart,
epicentre of absence.

Mr Slave Mentality walks away
towards a dark girl over yonder,
uttering,
'Chocolate Cake Chocolate Cake
Will you be my Chocolate Cake.'

Day for the dog

I sit here,
Goopa Bird,
and watch my people collected,
those who are slaughtered,
those who are slain,
be carried off
towards the wave of flame.

Their remains,
the evidence,
incinerated.
Numeration hidden: for fire leaves no fingerprints;

Guilt no more,
until the murderers too
are at death's door.

I watch him now,
lone white man,
whose only method of cleansing
was the Gun,
whose only means of bartering
was the bullet,

as he slips
towards the other side—

never imagining that they would return to greet him,
never imagining the murdered Long Pigs having souls.

As he slowly becomes more spiritual than secular,
this death day
being that for the dog.

There appear
round his deathbed,
faces and chanting
from earlier cullings.

He
screams!
yells!
begs!
for Mercy,

but finding none
where none was given,

he becomes
every flesh he ever wounded,
every emotion he extracted then ignored,
every scream not heard,

emanates
now
from his own throat,
and becomes the tormented
of every soul
he ever tortured.

The Sainthood of his peers
matters little now,
and the feebleness of his age protects him not,
as he realises too late what I the Goopa Bird already know,
for I have gathered many souls in my time:

That sins never die,
they just get older,
and
the
Spirit Seldom Forgets.

Love infected

Your skin,
softer than tears,
sends choruses echoing through my soul
        that would make birds weep and butterflies falter,

You,
my lover,
who leave lollipops and lullabies upon my dresser,
        a sweet sweeter than sweet,

The songs of sirens that needs no sound,
and an amour within the treasures of my chest,
        I have to whisper
        so the words trip over,

My expression a hushed monotone against the still
of night,
'I am worthy of your love,'

        and pinch myself,

        For could such love be so real?

Dear Siss,

It's Monday 5th July, it's overcast and the skies are emitting slight tears of concern, Tracey Chapman is playing and my tea is lukewarm. No sunny day, blue skies.

The camellia tree is in bloom; stark pink flowers of the rosebush stand out amongst the greyness of the day, the dogs play and shiver at the same time out on the verandah. They are not allowed in.

I'm considering my future, my purpose, my point. I have no job, no reason, no true life. At this point I am surrounded by tragedy, death thrice, funerals too. Rape, spinal injuries, alcoholism, misunderstanding and getting lost and losing sight of the real issue.

It's cold, but the rain fends off the ice—on the grass, but not in hearts and minds; defrosted only by substances, agony, joy, sometimes intertwined and inseparable, becoming one and the same.

An old black man down the road has just died, the black woman at the Point was raped a few weeks ago by her own cultural brothers. And I feel melancholy, unguided and without divine provision. What is this poison that has infected our minds?

And Tracey Chapman still strums and sings downheart.

My tea is cold. And sometimes I still consider suicide.

I want to walk, but it is raining and I have no umbrella. I love the rain and to let it soothe me, caress me, but dislike illness-induced debilitation less. I will sit, listen, and watch. Nature's sedative for the sad and thoughtful. They still think the boys should do the lawns and the girls should do the cooking and cleaning. My thinking is not here yet, so I stay silent, simply because I do not have the energy for arguments, however slight or severe exchange of opinions get.

And the boys get ten dollars more.

And I think of how I have always wanted fame, significance in the plurality, to rise from the dirt of the plain to stand on the mountain's peak; and how sometimes that peak is very distant. Sometimes to go around is easier than climbing.

But each morning I climb out of bed, each morning I rise, each new day I want to die happy, and each night I sleep, not wanting to know what tomorrow brings. And each day I live in the hope that I will make a difference for someone following—not just signatures in the sand to be erased effortlessly by an indifferent wind.

And they still line up with temporary dollars to win temporary fortunes.

And I've grown tired. And I am still young. It is just another day.

All my love,

Z.

The naked moon

The moon slapped her face
as she dared to reveal her black nakedness in lunar light,
the wind whipped frenzied
encircling her obedience
and the earth grappled with the soles
of her feet,
which were rough underneath,
knew not where they trod
but dared,
governed only by the desire to inherit any guidance
Creation kindly bestow upon her.
Her stomach,
rotund with realisation,
kept her company,
but not for much longer as she hurried towards that
unknown place
which would give her seed the sanctuary she desired for
herself.
The sweeping mamelons were plentiful with foliage
and fauna's abundance.
This may be the place, she thought, for her child to inherit.
She wanted to find where the moon and the sun
became one,
where the earth and the stars collided,
where the power of her would pass
into
the future.
And she thought about him
strong and stringy,
tall and just,
ebony caresses
and knew the world would be grateful for the fruit she
would bear.

His strong sharp teeth,
strong sharp mind,
although he was forbidden his own rebirth,
he was,
as their souls touched on her brief farewell,
Here.
Then the blinding
before her,
where the moon, the stars, and even the sun
shed tears of greeting
in their disrobing,
she knew this to be the place,
      her fate,
      her future.
On her knees in gratitude to the guiding spirit,
when from inside of her
the earth moved,
quaked,
ripped,
and spilt forth, gushing rivers of red—
volcanic life.
She did not scream or kick or cry
but smiled with pain
at the bark
held strong between her teeth,
absorbing any cries she may have uttered.
She threw her head back
and saw the world,
saw that she may live forever,
saw the future
fall from between her legs
and she for a moment
felt like the Goddess,
the Creator,
but knew the possibility of living forever
lay in her bloodied arms.

Diamonds on my plate

A beat in time
this heart of mine,
    and a thought that escapes into Neverland.

Where love is free
and the blind can see,
    and jail is a jealous Fool.

A shepherd's crook round my throat,
a paddle for a sinking boat,
    is all affection that attaches itself to Me.

There are children that are sometimes cold,
food that is sometimes gold,
    and you wanna make love Tonight?

Street kids murdered in the dead of night,
unlucky lives crushed by economic might,
    and you put diamonds on my Plate?

The young with stomachs rotund with tears,
the old with lives full of fear,
    and life becomes just Surviving.

The tourists roll in,
sex children accommodate sin,
    and you want to go to Bali?

Infants with mortars and missiles for their first Christmas gift,
a birthday that may never come,
    and love is just a Heartbeat.

Business heartless-beat condones
like an elephant with a fractured backbone,
    and you want new carpet for your Palace?

A glass of water for a drowning man,
building blocks and castles in the desert sand,
    and money does not make you Immortal.

A flood will not ease the drought,
bars do not keep evil out,
    and burnin ain't keeping Warm.

The earth will quake,
mountains will shake,
    and you are reminded your time is limited Here.

The callused stick of wanting

The black man's hand that grappled
with the callused stick of wanting,
which poked and prodded
at the spoiled and poisoned soils of his livelihood,
grew bloody.

No longer could he torment his physical and spiritual being
with the deception
that he mattered: that he was the fisherman
                    instead of the fish.

He roamed carelessly with intent,
inspecting what remained of his Dreamtime legacy,
the survival of which depended upon and was pitted against
the undulating heatwave of public opinion and policies.

The trees,
life-giving plants no longer,
had metamorphosed into commodity.

The water,
whose created purpose was to fulfil and nourish,
disappeared in the grime and filth
of progress.

Everything had been sold,
he knew,
to that persistent evil,
the monetary devil.

Pretty little china dolls

Pretty little china dolls
nice
all in a row
sit
upon her dresser.

Pretty little smiles
with cheeks
like
Persimmons.

Pretty little dresses
reveal no virtue,
and eyes
which see nothing.

Pretty little china dolls
nice
all in a row,

But blindness does not protect her
from the old man
down the road,
who stands
naked
as she passes by,
finding pleasure in revealing his only right to manhood.

Her only protection
is to turn her head and tell no lies—
his indecency;
her embarrassment,

Two decades
and nobody knows
why she is so rude
to the old man
down the road,

Turns her head
as she passes by.

Pretty little china dolls
sit
dusty and resigned
in a box somewhere,

Pretty little painted smiles parched,
and cheeks like
faded persimmons.

Poor man's wisdom

The common politician, small town education, experiencing
small town hypocrisy,
communication at its most simple.

Child speak
from
Adult thought,
whose language
and politics

are still

unsophisticated
unpolluted
and as of yet
to fail
or
enrich him,
establishing his own
cultural redoubt,
as entertaining and educating
as a clown at the circus,
interaction partitioned
emotions and pain
kept
Perfunctory.

Corners of her mind

Previously unoccupied corners of her mind
were now primarily concerned with the prospect
of being loved.

Love to her,
even though she was by all means
a mature woman,
was still relatively
a stranger.

She would shy away from any heart
reaching out,
recoiling at its prospective touch
and prospective warmth.
She didn't love easily
but rather
forcefully
and eventually,
regretfully.

There were those who looked upon her
as a darling bud of spring,
but to her,
she was continually hurt
by her own pricks.
Her mirror told truths
her mind's eye lied
every time.

Beauty in the eyes of others
is worthless
without
beauty in the eyes of self.
Such is the mirror of the abused.

Ode to Barbie

I never ever had a barbie doll complex,
simply because
I didn't look like her,
could never look like her,
but importantly,
now after years of trying,
did no longer want to look like her:
like turning Mother Theresa into Madonna
or vice versa,
I was more the raggedy anne type doll—
the natty hair
the round face
the soft, full, figure.
I had crucified myself for long enough
I had decided,
for being born me.

Sometimes I still have dreams of when I had long
blondish
hair,
until I awake
and realise
I never did have
long blondish
hair,
and then I try to run my fingers through
only to have them entrapped
in the thick
dreaded
masses,
and as I am still half asleep
I get frustrated
and try to rip out my locks,

my blackness,
but before I regain full control of my mind
I am momentarily sad.
When my mind regains full control of me
I am relieved
that this is not
noddy land,
and we all do not have to look like barbie,
anorexic bitch that she is.

I'd imagined that she would be the girl who sits at the front
of the class without a hair or piece of clothing where it
shouldn't be,
forever getting straight As
and eventually becoming class president or school leader,
while I
who sit at the back,
have got a runny nose and no hanky:
green sleeve,
can only look on in awe and envy,
wanting to know what it's like to be a barbie doll with a
vocabulary,
and the boy next to her,
Ken I call him, who is only half as interesting
but obviously her love interest.
I think
My God!
Barbie's even got a sex life,
I would kill for one of those!
But not with Ken,
which I'd imagine would be like staying home from school
and finding you have no one to play with,
it would kind've take all the fun out of it,
rolling over and seeing Ken there.

Then I start to wonder
Maybe this is noddy land and I'm in the wrong dream,

maybe we really are stuck under Jesus' frock
and still can't see his naughty bits,
like maybe somebody got the plots and characters confused,
like maybe there is a place on earth I can walk into
and be greeted by the words, 'What took you so long?'
or 'You're finally here!'
Being surrounded by what is seemingly perfection
kind've kills the ego a bit,
you know,
like pissing on a fire—
I bet barbie's never squatted under a tree out in the open
being one with nature,
too many creepy-crawlies getting where they shouldn't be,
and I look around the classroom
and there is no class in this room,
it's filled with creepy-crawlies
all vying for barbie's attention.

I am not your typical romantic interest,
it's like if all the girls were toilet cubicles and the boys
needed to go,
no one would be lined up outside mine,
not that that's a bad thing,
I decide,
looking at the buck-toothed, pimple-faced, saggy-arsed
egotistical clowns that they are;
in fact,
I know when I'm thirty
I will thank God that nobody was into raggedy annes
and none of that
Let's do it shit and tell no one!
Odd
they all knew I was odd
thankfully I wasn't the only one,
there were a few of us.
Curly Sue over there in the corner who always told jokes
nobody laughed at,

or Able Amos in the middle whose face was a permanent
ghostly white from staring at the computer so much because
he had no friends and who used to get perfect scores in
mathematics, but whose only
downfall was that he didn't look like Ken,
because Kens didn't have to be smart,
just as long as they were reasonably good looking.
Able Amos was more a roly-poly kinda kid,
but we didn't hang out together—
there was only one thing worse than a nerd
and that's a group of nerds,
so I started shirking off the other nerds who wanted
to hang with me,
not because I feared social suicide
but because the only thing we had in common was
our neediness,
our difference,
until I realised I had no one to talk to,
they didn't get my jokes and would never listen when I spoke.
So I stopped speaking,
then they said
how quiet I was,
how they didn't even notice when I was in the room.
It's not like I was ever here because I wanted to be,
rather
had no goddamn choice,
I was stuck for a while
couldn't choose my family or my friends
then it was
'Why don't you ever come out with us?'
Yeah right!
You'll find me at home sticking pins in my eyes
I used to drag my fingernails down the blackboard
to annoy them,
killed my fingers,

but God I used to enjoy watching them wince and squirm
kind've like they had on a loaded nappy,
or diaper if you're American.

Still,
when I last went home,
the barbie dolls had all gotten married
and were in the process of having little barbies,
Ken had a beer belly
which went well with barbie's permanent blue eye shadow
and permed bottle blonde hair,
she hadn't changed a bit.
Able Amos was very able indeed,
now owned his own business being boss to many Kens,
and I
wearing my black justice and AIDS awareness badges
was kind've conspicuous,
their eyes would seek out my political statements
which clashed with theirs—
which simply read FOSTERS—
then quickly avert,
seeking solace in familiarity,
like trying to count barbie's black roots or something,
and I felt like I was in a time warp.
Everyone who was anyone was still here
being no one,
except somebody's wife or husband,
identity in non-identity,
and I knew
that this raggedy anne
had finally found herself
in
herself,
and didn't need barbie's goddamn permission.

The things I never knew about you: me

I think it is with much regret
that I never knew you,
the colour of your eyes, the texture of your hair
or the shape of your mouth.

Yet it is your eyes I stare into when I look into the mirror,
your lips my lover kisses,
your nose all earthly aromas caress,
and my hands,
like yours I'm sure,
are so large and manly
which is of course
uncommon for a girl,
and my feet
were never dainty and I have never known why,
because they were so unlike my mother's,

So you see

I think it is with much regret
that I never knew you.

Forgive and forget

Sometimes images just fade
and you find yourself
wondering

whether it was real
or merely figments of our imagination.

And it is easy to forget,
if you are not reminded or educated
about past atrocities.

Mere wailings
of archaic ghosts
who live on in the flesh of presence,
who refuse to die

although focussed extermination

was the only purpose of a nation's existence

And yet the heart still Beats
and yet the blood still Circulates.

To forgive and forget is a fool's utopia—
Justice and Peace should persuade the rich man's pride.
Justice and Peace will convince the rich man's pride,

until all are equal
in truth
and all are equal
in life
as they are
in death.

My Tellurian grandfather

Harmony escaped
from black rounded lips
of my Tellurian grandfather

Voices sang,
telling of gospel feats,
I listened closely and could hear

Embedded within them,
ancient chanting
and stories of the beginning of time

Ancient corroborees,
ancient campfires,
black feet which stomped our mother earth

Clouds of red dust,
faces with terrestrial ochres:
cosmetic nature.

And although my grandfather stood before me
fully clothed,
I could see him in his natural state,
during the cosmos
of ancestral years,
long before he was stolen and given
Another
to worship.

'See the flame,' he would say, putting a hand to his chest,
'It always was and always will be.'

'But grandfather,' came my reply,
'you can put the flame out.'

'Yes,' said he,
'but there will always be fire.'

Hatred's shadow

Enforced cultural obsolescence
via policies
and institutionalised bigotry,
where prejudice is real
only between the lines,
and hatred
has no shadow.

Union

When the wave of instant like
and fear
and hesitation
has finally subsided
the calmer waters of repose wash over
creating emotion of
deepening like
impending friendship
and the union
of like spirits.

Genocide is never justified

And the past was open to gross misinterpretation.

Why do the sons and daughters of the raped and murdered
deserve any more or any less than those who have prospered
from the atrocities of heritage?
And why do the sons and daughters refuse to reap
what was sown
from bloodied soils?
And why does history ignore their existence?

This land, *terra nullius* was never barren and
unoccupied!

This land was never void of human life!

Instead
thriving with the knowledge of tens of thousands of years.

Everywhere I look!
Ghosts!

Vacant, colourless faces stare back

Sans culture
sans the belief of deserving of equality,

Who was here first is not the question
anymore

It is what you have done since you arrived,
the actions you refuse to admit to,
the genocide you say you never committed!

Then why are my people so few
when they were once so many?
Why is the skin so fair when once as black as the land?

Colonised Rape.

Why are you so rich, by secular standards
and we now so poor, by secular standards
The remnants of a culture though,
still

> *Rich*
> In
> *Spirit*
> and
> *Soul*

The neverending rain

Spiritual tenderness,
lust for dreams of past
boundaries of perception
of the last
universal, cumbersome
deeds of worth
apathetic fallacies of phallic forth
superior pious ponderous pain
emotional epicentre
of neverending rain.

These are the words bequeathed to me
these were to be my emotional sea
yet the legacy I could not fulfil
as the once beauteous heartbeat's beat is still.
All the days I studied at life
could not prepare me for the knife
that has been twisted and turned in my back and mind
and as I reach to see the hand that I held I find
that it is not the enemy foretold
but rather a trusted friend of old.

The friend I thought I knew to be well
the friend the secrets of my heart I would tell
but of whom the enemy was best made
out of the ruin of love and lust decayed
who could not bear to see me happy alone
yet my languor they could not condone
and every breath I breathe I breathe for me
and not for the one who would not notice my waving hand
as I drown in this
emotional sea.

Like white

Back straight and head held high
as you mouth the pride of Australiana
Yes You!
Black bitch and dirty black bastard
You!

as you take your place at your desk ready for your schooling
absorbing the miracles of the great white captain

> Cook?
> or Hook?

Whatever you may
whatever you say
you for now
believe,

because you are trying to be like everyone else,

Like White
Like normal

Like for now there is no prejudice
no   black   no   white,

until you do bad or do too good,
like excel   (for which you will be patronised)

or don't listen (for which you will be chastised)

as you start worrying about how your mother will pay her bills
or how she always affords to feed you
on next to nothing,

and not listening to God himself!

The teacher
the preacher

as he, in his eyes

tries to rescue you from savage ignorance
by delivering unto you the gospel,

the history books
the lies

and waits for you to speak them like they're truth,
like that's what really happened,
like captain cook really did discover australia.

Well I believed
until I saw the light,
but not before I was blinded by untruths or rendered
brain dead
by negative images of my predecessors,
until I believed I was a rescued savage
and that I should take great care in my pronunciation
of words
and my arithmetic,
so that I shall set myself apart.

I am not like the other savages,
I am now an   educated savage
I am now ready to try to be   normal

Like White.
Like what I say will make any difference
as to how you perceive me,

Like God preacher man

teacher man
don't look at me,

What if I am wrong?
and am still just a stupid black
Stupid Black!

Even if I know I am right,
my voice is frozen with the possibility of being wrong,
and not just a white wrong,
but a black wrong,
which is like ten times worse

So I stay silent,

and the preacher man
teacher man
no longer knows whether I have absorbed his lies

or whether

a blankness of mind replicates
the blankness of eyes.

Mask

She hid her face behind the veil of non-identity,
hoping that those who looked would not discover
her true self.
A lifetime had been spent
in the attempt of concealment.

It wasn't that she was ashamed
or afraid,
but would prefer the freedom of being a nondescript face
of the populace and what that entails,

of not having to fight for retribution,
of not having to struggle for some form of recompense,

Instead

renege the rights to culture,
deny the face of heritage,
accept the recidivisms committed
generation through generation,
and hope the offspring she would eventually bear
would betray her even less.

These were not the teachings from her mother's lips,
but were attributed
to environmental conditioning
of a much more powerful,
more persuasive ideal:

                    Society,

and what she thinks is surviving.

Mother

You
in all the years I have known you
have stood alone

apart

yet not without.

Your strength
was always silent,
so silent in fact,
my childhood ears could not recognise its simplicity,
and only in the impending wisdom of adulthood
have I begun to understand
how lucky I have been
to have come from your womb,
your seed,
which was never forsaken
or forgotten,
contrary to my earlier misconstrued belief,
when motherhood is sometimes mistaken
for perfection.
but knowing no one is beyond reproach.

And sometimes
the child shall teach,
and sometimes
the child shall show the way,
and understanding
that all love takes time
to comprehend and fulfil
and although I do not love easy,
it is getting easier to love.

Maybe Methuselah
(Mr Slave Mentality part II)

She knew God might be watching
and the angels too,
Peter Gabriel Moses
Solomon
and
Maybe Methuselah.

Her stomach turned violent,
her throat tormented,
and her mind
turned to thoughts of sin
for comfort.

beggar thief snatch cunt whore

cars on a cruise-by
deviates after dark

Are you working? he asked

Her pockets empty,
Her heart bleeding,
Her head fell
to her throbbing chest,

Will you be my Brown Sugar?

Her silence
became
his pleasure,
her impoverishment
became

his instrument
of power,
his

sword knife cannon tank bible

Her brown flesh
became a sin
of biblical
proportions.

Part the bastard

Smoke and alcohol fumes ascending,
clustered with the offspring
of the culturally mixed,
now
culturally connected.

Vulgar sights to many, these people,
        my brothers
        my sisters
who are spurned beyond these walls
and within,
but are welcomed
when money: temporary relief
                constant burden
leaves hand,
becoming briefly
        respectable
        acceptable,
momentarily
a part of
but still A—part.

Part
Black
part
White
part
Truths
part
Lies
part the Bastard
part the Damned
part the Chosen

part the Saved
part the Savage
part the Civil
part the Whiteman
part the Black
part the seas and let them drown
Yes,
these are
      part my brother
      part my sister
All
      My
            People.

Suicidal by nature

They gorged themselves on the fat of the land
'til it was lean and emaciated,
pillaging all that stood before them,
Man and Tree alike.

All were victims of spurious ethics
and sophist argument,
merely fly excrement in a paddock of cows—
of seeming insignificance.

However,
the inconsequential insect would prevail,
where the greater beast,
ample as it was,
would eventually be consumed by its own vicious
dependency,
felled by the duality—

Thus returning to the sterile dust
it created.

A Dreamtime awakening

to this peculiar progressive secularity,
forsaken for Christian charity,
for only one chosen God is just
and in him we trust,
for my brothers and sisters we must
reject our material lust.

And if they kill in His name
it is not the same
as murder.

Instead

let it be renamed spiritual liberation
to tame primitive moral desecration,
for they are interested in only
the capturing of souls,
worth more than the gold
that our ancestors told

us never to touch.

And let the Christian God live!
In tears
and fears

so that should anyone kill in another god's name
it is the same
as murder.

What kind of people?

You shake your head in disbelief,
announcing your ancestors could never be capable
of such murderous feats.

What kind of people would kick the heads off babies
or rip at the stomach of the impregnated,
as would a ravaged wolf,
or castrate the manly,
all in the name of civilising

the uncivilised?

What kind of people would dig at the earth
committing sacrilege,
ripping the very life from her core and at the same time,
ripping the very life from their own,

all in the name of progress?

And what kind of people would elect themselves as the
supremacist race
by virtue of the christened barrel,
all in the name of peace

and justice?

And what kind of people would hold one man's name aloft,
and say   those they slay,
               they slay for him!

And those who do not do as they do,
do
evil.
What kind of people?
What kind?

Poverty is silence

Is it still just a matter of principle
to disconsider
the few
while
tolerating
plurality?

The only strength of reasoning
being in
the
number,

The only truth
being in
monetary power,

For Money Speaks
and poverty
is silence,
and silence can mean
death,
if you accept and obey

Without question.

Rushin' rule-ette

When my brother was twelve years old,
the local police played Russian roulette
with him,

pressing the cold hard barrel
to his young temple,
young mind

        and clicked!

Now
the pistol is a shotgun
aimed at his back,
as he flees for dear life

        that explodes!

Now
the pistol is an almost empty bottle of port,
as he fends off the winter—and society's
coldness

        that confuses,

Now
the pistol is empty pockets and an empty outstretched hand
as he tries to afford his own existence

        that shatters,

Now
the pistol is an inviting noose made of shoelace,
as he contemplates sleep,
and rest,
and maybe peace

forever.

And now
the Constable is a Sergeant as he reprimands a junior
saying such racist attitudes are unnecessary,

until

they are alone.

Womankindness

She is trying to get out
She is trying to get out
She is trying to get out

This woman inside of me
This woman inside of me
This woman inside of me

She is ready to come out
She is ready to come out

This woman inside of me
This woman inside of me

Like the worm ready to be removed from the heart
of the blossoming rose,

Like the growing green tree snake,
ready to forsake its marred and scarred,
used and abused
skin,

Like the delinquent sparrow ready to abandon
its alienated nest
and soar on the breath of creation,

far from here
far from here

and there is no turning back.

Like the butterfly choosing once again
to become the grub,

Like the frog relinquishing,
choosing once again to be the tadpole,

Like the hearing
choosing to be deaf,

Like the sighted
choosing to be blind.

She has seen too much now
this woman inside of me,

to be ever the   misinformed,
                        menial,
                        meek,
dutiful courtesan again.

She instead

Will rejoice in her Womankindness.

Truganini or piccaninny

Truganini you call me, or piccaninny,

and should want that I take offence,
but I choose not to, as Truganini,

in my Herstory books anyway,
was not a bad person.

Like a flame taking offence at being called
fire,
or
the Pope taking offence at being called
a believer.

Black bitch you call me,
and you should want that I defend myself:

Yes, I am Black,
to use your language.

Bitch?

Well you are allowed your misogynistic opinion
to which I pay no heed,
for I am not interested in the words that fall
from the mouths of fools,
as I am tired of you choosing stereotypes

and who
Shall,
and
Shall not

be my role models,

and who
Does
and
Does not

appeal to the anglo aesthetic.

I am a
Black
Woman,

regardless of any name you dare to say
as it is superfluous,
and I shall not adopt your derogatory undertones

simply!

because they come from your utterance, your mentality,
your state of being.

As
you have the ability to say
Aboriginal,
and make it sound like
Dog.

I am not a dog.

You have the ability to say
Black,
and make it sound like
Evil.

I am not evil.

You have the ability to say
Woman,
and make it sound like
Whore.

I am not a whore.

But
I
Am
A
Black
Woman.

So

Black, Nigger, Coon, Djin, Truganini or Piccaninny,

how I identify

Is!   Up!   To!   Me!

You are Black?

If you are oppressed in any way,

you are Black.

If you are a woman who loves women
or a man who loves men,

you are Black.

If it is that people do not accept you
simply for what you do,

you are Black.

If they do not accept that their God is not yours
or yours is not theirs, and would want to crucify,

you are Black.

And should your thoughts be your own
and you dare to differ,
for one who is strong is not afraid of standing alone,
you know what it is

to be Black.

And should they attempt to
silence your voice
or
remove your rights,

you have glimpsed
the gestapo,

the gas chambers,
the enforced cultural emaciation,

you have felt the searing nullity of the branding iron,
forecasting nirvana,

for you know what it is to fight
for the simple right

to exist

As You Please.

Taxi driver

I've got thirty seconds to explain two hundred years of oppression and display apparent alacrity to justify *why* my people *still* camp under trees? The taxi driver, professor, master, politico common, says he is right. That he is the endangered species, he is the people who have been dispossessed, taken from their Mother Land. Go back, I say.

Why do you deserve any special recognition? he asks rhetorically, taking a sip of coffee from the Holy Grail. I start to speak and cannot stop because history is complex and socio-economic warfare unfair and my thirty second time slot is thrice over and the meter has stopped and I've just begun, and as he, the knight, drives off into the night on his great white steed, at great white speed, I know I have converted no one, and that unbeliever   leaves an   unbeliever.

Cultural incursion

From a mountain's crest I view
the cultural incursion
where jewelled oceans
no longer protect
from the windswept beasts
but rather
on the perilous waves of stratagem
approaches what is
for my mob
the end
of
Peace.

The universe within

The winds will keep blowing,
and the sun
will continue to both nurture and condemn
the crusted earth,

mortal bodies will either be fattened by the undulating
disposition of their surroundings,
      or depleted,

the waves will wash weary shores
of barren and forsaken island paradises
long after the final breath has escaped from my lips.

So what is the purpose of being? I ask myself
during moments of tormented insomnia,
hounded by both conscious and unconscious actions to
cement my inert desire to belong and be needed

        either to the masses,
        ideally to the individual,

or better still
      both.

The mountains that have survived centuries
of environmental torment,
nature's punches and caresses,
will not be moved
should I on the morrow
find my feet planted no longer on the soil
but rather,
beneath it.
The birthing will continue,

as will the dying
and the killing

of things old and new,

young lives will be cut short,
old lives brought to an abrupt end.

And still I watch,

waiting for signs from above, preferably above,
as that is where they tell me divinity lives,
and that all evil lurks beneath and at the core
of the dusty landscapes.

But how could the core of life conceal such evil?
How could the Mother entomb such spiritual deformities?

That is when it becomes quite clear
the universe is not out there,
        but rather
        within.

I cannot conjure the desire to know the beginning of time,
would prefer to know,

Why I am afraid of loneliness? and am scared by my own
lack of appetence?
Why I cannot love?
Why I prefer solitude?

For the universe will exist
as it always has
regardless

whether I know   or not.

Raggedy Anne

Even when we were young we were taught it was impolite
to dissuade the drunken,
or even sober
abated sentiments,
the open arms of an uncle
(or any male member of the family,
or maybe even just a dear family friend)
whom we were taught to respect
regardless,
that we,
the young
vulnerable female,
should go forth and be bounced
upon his strategically positioned,
child entertaining,
child penetrating
knee,
and pretend to like it.

Smile little girl
smile
like a Raggedy Anne
or a
Poppet,
Floppet,
or whatever the hell kind of doll you care
to name,
for like Raggedy Anne
and Poppet
and Floppet
I was never heard,
for being a child meant having no rights to choose,
to say

Yes
I will
or
No
I won't
or
Yes
I do
or
No
I don't.

And that was in the protected light of day
when we were all enjoying being what was considered a
normal
nuclear
caring tearing
family,
but what about when the reality of day
becomes
nightmares of night,
what about when those open arms turn
into cold,
unwelcome
hands
of sandpaper,
in the heavy
lonely
forsaken
still darkness?

When there is only my
heartbeat
thump thump thumping,
and the sound of blood

and fear
rush rush rushing
to keep
me company,
and I imagine
I am not here
but some other place
and I stare
at the map of the world at the end of my bed,
I become very good at geography,
knowing the countries
and their capitals
and where I would rather be
in the world,
but still
he is here,
and there would be nothing more that I would like
than to scream
loud!

But my throat is frozen
and my breath
shortened
for fear has fastened its phallic fist
tightly
round my throat,
and his
knife for a finger
cuts right through me,
gun for a penis
stone for a heart
mephitic breath,
stench which makes me want to vomit.
I wish the animal,
who is less than a dog that is motivated only by instinct,
dead!

I would lay awake
amidst the predatorial darkness
in the decade to come
plotting his murder.
Should it be possible that a fourteen-year-old girl
could kill
a grown man
and remain
free?

I don't kiss the
lips
or the arses
of
uncles fathers brothers or others.
In his mind
time has paid homage
to his conscience, and the statutory time limit for guilt
has passed
and eased.
He has redeemed his innocence
whereas I,
in the dark recesses of my mind
still pay the price
and
as a consequence,
I am sentenced to a lifetime of never being able to forget
for his Crime.

Mamillates and tresses

She looked into the sky
and had never seen it blue,

but she always saw Women in the Trees,

Wooden mamillates carved by the hand of nature

abdomens
     sleek
          gnarled
               and aged,

torsos
     willowy
          slender
               and smooth,

all with the offer of comfort

their limbs
          reaching skyward,
               guiding spirit
                    reaching outward,

spread like a perennial cloak over the land.

With the dark advancing,
her concealed form would weave
in
and
out,
their long green dresses and tresses,
which protected her

from the disobedience of night,

and the moon,

        smiling and
        guiling her,

brought with it
        the pain

of bad spirits that would be expelled from her body
each time,

and she cursed,
knew
it was the weight
of her woman.

The males,
big thoughts and bold opinions,
big spears and calculated hunting,

would not miss her for some time

then with eyes and mouths simpering
and the emotion of life high,
the smell of fresh meat still on their breath,
would maybe seek her.

It was time for her to dwell
amongst the woman trees,
who built homes for the young,
provided food for the hungry,
shelter for the lost,
and whose milk
seeped from pores when wounded,

For they came
armed with fire and stone,
and tore from the core

Flesh

upon which they would float
and bring back creatures
from the deep,
the wooden phalanx that could be thrown
as far as the eye could see,
and the hollowed and burnt shell of her flesh
that would allow the men to echo their existence
across all the land,

the voice of man and tree combined.

She would sit there and speak with the woman trees,
asking them stories of the Dreamtime
for they had seen much,
and had witnessed the passing of many.
She would inquire
who were the spirits that lived in their branches
that sung each time she passed by,
whispering her name?
Nunkerri! Nunkerri!
Come be with us!

So
she became known
as the protector of trees.

For many years to come,
her people would see her amongst the leaves—
neither shape nor form,
just shadow,
and she would converse with the birds

that resided there,
and the small animals of fur
who were sometimes sacrificed
for the warmth
of man.

The moons of time would pass,
she had seen the trees naked
and adorned
many seasons,
her mortal flesh had begun to wither where theirs did not,
she lay on her bed
of fallen leaves
that became her burial.

Her people had moved on
to the hunting grounds with plenty
and she,
who had no friends
that moved,
that were not committed
to the earth,
remained.

They returned
moons later
to the place of stomping,
and say she still be there,
for in the darkness
was the ghost tree,

bark as pale as the flashing lights
that sometimes appeared
in the midnight skies above,
commanding both fear and respect for
the ghost of the woman protector.

Her trunk
　　　svelte and soaring
　　　　　　sleek and skyward,

with the wind offering her speech, as she foretold
things to come,

stood with,
and watching over
her people,
who danced

among them.

This place

There is a place where babies are more burden than beauty,
where education is an empty cause, and sport to the able is
the only way out.

> A one-horse town that needs just a pub
> and a post office,
> and in the middle,
> a station for the police.

Where reading means just being able to sign your name,
and arithmetic becomes obsolete, except when counting
small change.

> Where the blacks are bludgers
> and women are whores
> and alternative thought
> is a foreign notion.

Where art is only for aristocrats, love is confused with
desperation, and marriage is often a last resort.
Where social security day brings excitement,
'cos jobs are few and far between, and holidays are a two-
dimensional fantasy.

> Where one parent families
> are more common than not,
> brothers and sisters only half,
> but it still means being a family.

The old remember all, for time drags her feet, while the young lay with hands behind their heads supine, swearing to never end up like the rest, their only true desire

Is to get out of This Place.

Singer Songwriter

Alf Taylor

Alf Taylor was born in Perth in the late 1940s. He spent his younger years with his family in Perth, then joined his brother in New Norcia Mission. Alf spent the rest of his childhood there. As a young man he worked around Perth and Geraldton as a seasonal farm worker. He joined the Armed Forces and was based at various locations around Australia. Alf then left the Armed Forces and went home. After a marriage, seven children (only two of whom survived) and a divorce, Alf Taylor found his voice as a writer and poet...although it is a gift he believes he was born with.

Alf has released two poetry collections with Magabala Books. *Singer Songwriter* was published in 1992, *Winds* in 1994. All of the poems contained in *Singer Songwriter* are republished in this collection.

Contents

To my three granddaughters,
Jasmine, Danita and Rhianne.

Black skin

Warm sun on black skin
warm soil under black skin
black skin burns
black skin learns
black skin hangs.

Black skin in fear
black skin can't hear
black skin feel pushed
black skin thinks bush.

Black skin with wine
black skin thinks
life not mine
black skin balance on line.

Ancestors cry from afar
black skin head for bar
black skin feel no pain
black skin drunk again.

Black skin see no tomorrow
black skin head in sorrow
black skin fight
black skin see no right.

Black skin cry
black skin die
black skin no hope
black skin grabs rope.

You are

You are a
cool gentle breeze
on a
hot summer's day.

You are
a warm fire
in the
freezing month
of May,

A warm sun
on a
cool morn,

A trickle
of water
to a
parched throat.

On a
placid lake
you are
a boat.

It is
only me
who could see
in my mind.

Sunlight

Standing
on the
edge of darkness
I just
do not
know
what to do.

People are
beckoning me
from the darkness.
I turn
to see you
standing
in the bright
sunlight.

You are
screaming
my name
as I turn
to run
and to
hold you tight.

Moment of paradise

Stolen glances
fleeting
lock of eyes
moment
of paradise.

No
words spoken
chemistry flow
a smile
hearts
beat wild.

The hit

Cascade
of tears
brain
overflow
with fear.

Tightening
of a syringe
prick
of a needle
rejuvenation begin.

Float
into space
play
amongst the stars.

Flare
of vibrant colours
explodes
in his mind.

Tomorrow
awake
in cold sweat
and sorrow

Screams
and screams
for a needle
and a syringe.

Sleepless nights

Sleepless nights
the storm in my head
I want to cover
rolling of waves
head does not want to discover.

Silently drinking
silently thinking
silent thoughts of sleepless nights.

Darkness wakes the mind
the body does not make a sound
thoughts of yesterday
erupt in volcanic disruption.

Love

Let
Today be fine,
Tomorrow it can rain
as I hold
your warm body
next to mine.

Your lips
are inviting
your skin
so soft and smooth.
Your smile
ever so tender
as your hand
clasped in mine.

I could
drink from your cup
filled so much
with love.

So let it be fine
as you gently
press your lips
to mine.

A love affair

Come on in
Let life begin
Behind closed doors
Let our fantasies soar.

A discreet meeting
Between two adults
A love affair
That should not
Be there.

I was the instigator
You were the participator.
At times I feel
This is not right

So I am going to gently Disappear
From your life
And glide silently
Back to my wife.

She

She was
a single mum
whose life
was shattered
by divorce.

She picked up
the pieces
with a child,
she did not
let her
imagination run wild.

Endless
flow of bills
greeted her
each day

As she
gallantly attempted
to find her way.

The petal

Softly
the rose petal
falls to the ground.
Gentle breeze
tosses it
around and around.

Uneven
cobblestones
tear at its
skin.

Bruised and battered
it starts
to cry.
Caught in the brush
it eventually
dies.

The flats

She left
from here
in quiet despair
never more
to return.

These flats,
she said,
are driving
me mad.

With a bowed
head
she whispers,
Yet leaving
my friends
makes me feel
so sad.

A dream

Shrouded
by the darkness
of the night

Your body so close
I wanted to
hold you tight.

I glanced at your face
it looked aglow
your pouting lips
I wanted
to get to know.

A mist of sadness
engulfed me
as you
got up to go.

I awoke
with a start.
Yet again
it seemed
that you
were only
a dream.

Bring back

Gone is the rainbow
from the sky,
gone is the bird
that can't fly,

Gone is the willow
that can't cry,
gone is the wind
that can't sigh,

Gone is a love
I should have tried.
People I know
are on my side.

I'm fed up
with swimming against the tide,
no longer am I going to hide.

Break the shackles
from your heart,
Arise with the sun
for a brand new start,

Bring back
the rainbow to the sky,
bring back
the bird that can fly,

Let the wind
make the willow cry
as it rustles the leaves
with a sigh.

Fitzroy bed

I see them
all before me
sitting on
the dry Fitzroy bed.
What if
I make a mistake?
was running through my head.

Eager eyes upon me
as I told
of long ago,
the dark
smiles across their faces
gave me
a pleasant glow.

I talked and talked
until
the hot Fitzroy
sun went down.
When I finished
everyone was clapping
and a few were moving around.

I'll never forget
that day.
It will always
be in my head
how they listen intently
on that dry
Fitzroy bed.

Black child

Little black child
as you play
you seem forgotten.

Forgotten like the stories
your father
used to hear
Forgotten like the spear
as bibles appear.

Forgotten like the elders
who tell
of long, long ago
Forgotten like the people
who still
do not wish to know.

But you
little black child
do not grow up wild.
Listen to the elders
as they tell
of long, long ago.

Look at the spear
as it travels through the air.
Into a young man
you grow.
Look after the elders
with care.

Little black child
if you listen and learn
you will never be forgotten.
Wherever you go
the elders will always know.

Pension day

Good mother all week
dignified she keeps.
Baby feels the change
Pension day in range.

Pretty dress on
she carries baby along.
She knows what they'll say
Today is pension day.

Town alive
with pretty clothes.
Baby knows
as mother goes.

Food will be bought
cheap clothes sought.
Better put money here
gotta have a beer.

Pub is loud
mother look proud.
There'll be dancin
and a lotta romancin.

Sun goin down
baby looks around.
Mother sways
effect of pension day.

Baby cry
mother staggers on by.
See how she sway
end of pension day.

Town

Green leaves on trees,
what I like to see,
wind blowin in my face,   .
my mind I like to erase
town with no grace.

Shadows of past goin by,
life of stress must start,
brush the cobwebs from your heart.

Looking into life of pain,
being caught in the rain,
reserve full of memories,
town full of gain.

Today's tribe thinking of past,
a yacht with a broken mast,
water comes into the bow.
Pick up a spear
and ask ... how?

Peace all around,
sits in a humpy,
doesn't make a sound,
picks up a paper
and starts to read:
Russia has taken the lead.

A rifle he hunts prey,
humpy he wants to stay,
highway comin by,
town he must try.

Train noise coming afar,
drives down highway
in his flash car.

Alone in a cell

Here I sit in this darkened cell
my head is so heavy
and my body not well.
Been on the plonk for a month or two
my brain so screwed up
I don't know what to do.

A night alone in this cell I dread
being closed up I may as well be dead.
If only I can live through the night
I'm sure tomorrow's gunna be alright.

As the hours pass by I start to see
the devils and monsters are laughing at me
Why didn't I pay that ten dollar fine?
then these devils and monsters wouldn't be mine.

If I do something real bad
I know all my relations will be sad.
If only they'll open the door
I just can't take it no more.

I look at the towel and it looks like a rope
I've got to get it, my only hope.
Noose around my neck I jump to the floor
I hear the distant noise of a key in the door.

Then a voice so far away
seems like it's coming from yesterday:
Get him down get him down
we've got to bring him round.

I often think back as the years go by
What made me attempt to give that stupid act a try?
May all the spirits of my ancestors above me
guide me through the remaining years of my life.

Kimberley

In my flat
looking
out of
my window

Thinking
of the
Kimberley

Where
my heart
longs
to be

Warm sun
of
ultraviolet rays
languishing
in the
misty haze
of those
warm sunny days

Setting sun
of
blood and gold
Stairway
to the moon
longing
to go
back soon.

Words

The embers
of their young hearts
silently glowed
the smile on their faces
clearly showed.

The old fella
told the children
of long time ago.

The children
listen intently
grasping every word.

Dare not
to make a sound
as the words
gently flow
around and around.

My mind

In my mind I see
gold and diamonds surround me,
standing around a shroud
or floating on a cloud.

My mind is my travel agency,
it takes me to any place I fancy,
it makes me write a fancy verse
or lets me explore the Universe.

I really appreciate my mind
when my body's in a bind
with it, I can become King
or with a voice of honey I can sing.

My mind is so free,
I can be what I want to be,
no obstacle too strong,
no road is too long.
In my mind I can do no wrong.

Or when I feel like tossing it in
it makes me fight like hell to win,
it tells me I'm just me.
It always brings me back to reality.

King of the Kimberley

A lack
of understanding
that goes on today,
complete ignorance
in society
I would say.

Aboriginal culture
has to be
taught in schools today.
We were always told
of Captain Cook
sailing on his
merry way.

Even Ned Kelly
in a conversation
always held sway.

Why not talk about Pigeon
in his feats of bold,
always leaving the troopers
standing out
in the cold.

Soldier Pigeon

Soldier
of fortune
Soldier
of fame
Soldier
of the
highest regard
Soldier Pigeon
who rode
the Kimberley Range.

Sniffin

Why
do you sniff glue
they asked?

I don't know
I reply
Maybe I'll forget tomorrow.

In our household
there is
a lot of sorrow,

Nan is sick
Mum cannot cope
and Dad
he is drunk again.

I have
got so little space
and yet
so much time,

I sometimes wish
this life
not mine.

I wish I had
a lotta schoolin
then
this stupid sniffin
I won't be doin.

So I will
probably sniff glue again
to get away
from that shadow
of pain.

The trip

Lifting the bottle
to his parched lips
the revolting liquid
his hungry throat
did not want to miss.

With a grunt and a groan
into an empty well
the dirty brown liquid
fell like a stone.

The warmth in his blood
started to flow
eyes glazed
words become slow

Floating into universe
warm sun explodes
into a cascade of brilliance
of flowing fun.

Where did I go wrong?
he gently weeps
resting his head
on the evening star
as he goes into a blissful sleep.

Dole cheque

Dole cheque comes today
I wish that I could steal away
all the Nyungars will be around
gotta get away without making a sound.

Nyungars will head to the pub
that's where they'll find me
sitting quietly here
having a beer.

They'll be asking for a price
I'll give but it won't be nice
cheques don't last long today
I may as well give or they won't go away.

Grab a carton and a flagon
and head for the bush
before the Munnaritj
give us the push.

A drunken voice will say
'Hey that's not right,
you got my woman.
Me and you gunna fight.'

Sun comes up bodies go down
black eyes and love bites
as I look around
holding my head in pain
I can't wait for the dole cheque again.

No names

The chains
of silence
have been
broken

By a
Death
in Custody
the word
has been
spoken.

Who is
to blame?
Who is
to blame?
Lots of questions
but no names.

Is it
a game?
No one
is to blame.
A lot
of questions
but still no name.

Lightning Man

Lightning Man strike your light
Across the darkness of the night,
Lightning Man let me hear you
Crack with old man thunder,
Lightning Man please listen to what
I have to say.

Lightning Man along with your clouds
Bring relief to this parched land,
Lightning Man beat the clouds into submission,

Lightning Man make them weep, weep and weep,
Lightning Man so electrifying so strong,
Lightning Man to me you can do no wrong.
Thank you for the tears of rain.

Makin it right

I'll try and make things right
through writing and poetry
I just might
but we'll all have to pull together.
Never mind how far apart
someone somewhere gotta make a start.

informal

With all this bickering amongst black and white
character assassination gives me a fright
if we can't say anything nice to each other
let's not talk, then it's no bother.

ignorance = bliss or civility?

When I was a kid there was no colour.
As I got older I found there's black white and yellow.
Who cares about the colour?
It's the person inside that matters.

Let's stop calling each other names,
get into a huddle and start playing the game.
There's only one thing for me
it's winning and winning and being free.

I know that's only a dream of me and you
but if we put our heads together it could come true.
Never mind how far apart
someone somewhere gotta make a start.

Racial tension in 02

112 *Alf Taylor*

Old Blue

I looked down at him,
yes he was getting old.
No more catching roos, I said.
Old Blue dropped his head.

When he was a pup
by his graceful motions
Dad could tell
that he was going to kill well.

When Dad took him out
Mum would make a damper,
knowing in her heart
Old Bluey would kill from the start.

When food was scarce
Old Bluey would provide.
We could see when he'd killed a big boomer
by the scratches on his hide.

As spotlights and rifles began to stalk the prey
Dad would always say,
Give me a good roo dog any day.

High powered cars and bikes,
Old Blue gradually lost his bite
but to us he was always our shining light.

One morning we found that Old Blue had passed on by.
At times our family would cry
for a wonderful roo dog somewhere in the sky.

Debbil Man

The Debbil Man
I see
in the darkness
is beckoning me.
Come... come
I hear
the chilly night wind calling.

I know
what the tribe
will say: Keep away, keep away,
for him bad.
You go to him
we all be sad.

They say
he will
take your spirit
your body and your soul.

He Debbil Man
that one, pull blanket
over
your head.
And don't listen
to what
the Debbil Man
said.

The mission

After prayers at night I go to bed
lying awake with memories in my head.
I can still see my mother kneeling on the ground
sobbing, Don't take my child, I want him around,

When the Native Welfare came and took me away.
Even now at times I still cry inwards and say
I belong to a tribe, honest and just,
not a religion, we live by a must.

Not in a mission, but I'd rather be
hugging my mother, sitting on her warm bended knees.
For one day I'd like to tell the world
how the missionaries put my brain in a whirl.

I tried my best to play along with their rules
praying and praying and going to school.
Being a blackfella was my only tool,
doing things for Jesus and keeping my cool.

I know one day I'll be free,
free from religion and free from rules.
Free to make up my own mind and free to be cool
but I know the damage has already been done
as I see myself lying drunk in the hot morning sun.

Rules

I looked
at the figure
before me

It was dishevelled
and trembling slightly.
The cracks
on his face
I would have
loved to erase.
Death was approaching
but he
did not want me
to know.

With a quiver
in his voice
he turned to me
and said,

Once boy
our ancestors
were free
in this beautiful land.
Now
I don't understand.
So many rules so many rules
blackfellas
owning the jails
still cannot own land.

With tears
in my eyes
I watched
him shuffle away.
Looking
at his bent back,
I openly cried
and whispered
I love you Dad.

Goodbye.

In memory of Kevin 'Doc' Humphries

from Alma

Oh Doc
I can see the darkness
on a bright sunny day
since you
were laid to rest
on that hot summer's day.

I can still see your coffin
being lowered down.
My heart openly wept
knowing you will
never be around.

You was
a gun shearer
in the past
until gerbah
took its toll.
I felt you would not last.

Now I look back
on the good times we had.
With you away shearing
I always felt sad.

When you
got back to the camp
it was always great.
With pound notes
in your hand

you would grab and kiss me
saying, 'Here you are mate!'

You used
to keep me awake
playing Slim Dusty's tapes
ever so loudly.
You would listen
to them proudly.

Now
I feel like a shell
but I still
got my memories
of you, dear Doc.

Fight

Had to fight since the day I was born
on that cold winter morn,
not only for life but for dignity
in today's society.

I had to fight every inch of the way
to get where I am today
around drunken fights
surrounded by drunken nights.

Dole cheque every fortnight
was my only shining light
but after long last
I really was going nowhere fast.

Put myself in gear
decided to get away from here
fed up with drunken nights
headed for the city lights.

Not quite grasping the straw
with determination I pushed for more.
Support from friends was overwhelming
sunlight was just beginning.

Fair skin boy

Wrenching
of a heart,
killing
of joy,
being parted
from her
fair skin boy.

Agonising years
river of tears
emptiness
all around.

Lived
with hope
one day
she will
see
her fair skin boy.

Chance
on a street
she did meet
her fair skin boy.

Mother

My dear kind, sweet and loving Mum

I can't understand why
for such a gentle woman to pass on by.
I always thought you would live forever
I thought, death to you never.

I know roses bloom then die
I know the grass go brown with no rain
but when they told me that you died
all I felt was pain.

So farewell and not goodbye Mum
Your body is gone but not your spirit.
My love for you will be shouted aloud
so wherever you are you will hear it.

I feel your presence all around
and sometimes I feel it on the ground.
Your patience, love and understanding,
your rules never hard and demanding.

I will leave your freshly mounded grave
knowing all your life you gave.
In my heart there is no other
only the memory of you dear Mother.

The fine

He talked
about the time
when the police
picked him up
for a lousy fine.

Ten dollars fifty he said
as he
unintelligently scratched
his head.

Locked away
with murderers, rapists,
child abusers
and bum bandits.

When the time
was up
they unlocked the door.
He went so fast
the coppers never
seen him no more.

A price

He told me
when he was a young boy
he was always
on the roam
never quite stayed
in one place
long enough
to call it home.

Cheap wine
and a park bench
was his only
gift to life.
Maybe, he said,
things might
have been different
if
I would have
taken a wife.

But I am
too old now
to worry about the past
I just live
for today,
tomorrow can take care
of itself.

So please
give me a price my friend
cause I do not care
if my life
is at an end.

No hope

I have
seen it before
and I see it now.
How far will it go
before
someone walks through
the door?

The haze
of alcohol
lingers in the air.
The smell of
sweaty bodies
and the stench of dope.
These are the people
of no life
and no hope.

Last ride

Neon lights
were beckoning him
as he hit
the street that night.

Little did he know
what was in store.
He would never be
patrolling the streets
no more.

His friends
in a stolen car
pulled up.
Jump in, they yelled,
we're going for a spin.

Drinks in the car
as neon lights
flashed past.
They heard the wailing sound
of sirens at last.

Thrill
of the chase
power of the car
police beaten by far.

Driver
not realising
he was at a bend on a hill.

Crunch
of twisted metal
then everything was still
for all five teenagers
in the stolen car were killed.

Gerbah

People on gerbah going nowhere fast
think people don't drink are coming last.
Little they know these people who go slow
always sure of knowing just where they go.

I heard him say, with drunken pride,
Tellin me gerbah no good they gotta hide,
tellin me about gerbah. I'm a man.
No one tells me, I'll drink all I can.

Today he'll enjoy life and have all the fun.
The time he's forty body wrecked his life nearly done.
Dead brain cells and a burnt out liver,
lays in a cold sweat and starts to shiver.

Lying in a hospital doctors all around
Why didn't I listen? he thinks. He doesn't make a sound
When I was younger should've slowed down a pace.
No use cryin, I think I've run my race.

Message Mum gets, he has died today
She's upset and quite dismayed.
Why didn't my boy slowen down, she sobs,
Not drinkin around with all his mob?

With no schoolin what have they got?
A dole cheque and a bottle, that's what.
Schoolin is a must for today
For the kids so that they can help pave the way.

We blackfellas

We say there is hope for tomorrow
but we blackfellas
are still living in sorrow.
We are trying to make a life.
The media always keeps us in strife.

Never of good things
we do.
The media will always punish
me and you.

We blackfellas are trying
to stand tall.
Our enemy the media
are always making us fall.

We have been stripped
of our pride.
The media have got a hide.
We blackfellas must stand
as one
as the fight still goes on.

'88

With Prince Charles opening the year
the blackfella still living in fear,
I can understand all the fuss it caused
'88 I look back on with remorse.

Black Deaths in Custody was the main topic.
The man at the top said he was going to stop it.
More money was the order of the day,
this giving the authorities more power to flay.

Bombing and killing were oh so ripe,
bank robbers making their daily swipe,
drugs and prostitution was always a point,
kids roamin the street sucking a joint.

Deaths on roads were oh so frequent,
with random breath testing they tried to end it
but faster the car the deadlier the weapon
as another mangled wreck lay out in the open.

Death and destruction number one of the year,
another woman raped, bashed and living in fear.
With hunger pains in its belly, the little child
screams in mother's ear
as mums and dads quietly shed a tear.

I just hope things are different in '99
as we all advance hand in hand in a horizontal line.
Maybe if we all prayed to the almighty above
to give those two terrible Ds a shove.

Wall of darkness

Feel safe
within the wall of darkness.
No one
can touch me
no one can see,
only me.

I see a tribe
who's solemn and sad.
I see infighting,
it makes me feel so bad.

I see my ancestors
rise from the dead
so proud
so strong
the chains
around their necks
so heavy, so long.

Across their chest
is a message
written in blood:

We died
that you could live
we died
that you could give.
Leave the bottle alone
if not
the lizards
will leave only bone.

Then I see
the spirit of my mother
looking for me.

Her face
has a saintly glow
she is at peace
and she knows

No more
being torn apart
by her fair skin
from the start.

I have
got to come out
from this wall of darkness

Where people can see,
people can touch me.
I won't accept it
but I have to
come back to reality.

Dreams

Oh for the dreams
I had last night
some were scary
some were bright.

I dreamt I held your hand
but I couldn't understand
that your hair was red
and your body dead.

You floated above me
you told me you loved me
you looked like the morning star
shining from afar.

Then I dreamt we slept in a bed of roses.
People said they didn't know us.
I'm sure I was the King
laying without the Queen.

I didn't want to surrender to the dawn
as I awoke to the chill of the morn,
laid back and tried to capture that dream.
Not likely it seems.

Leave us alone

I wish these do-gooders would leave us alone
for we have been forty thousand years on our own.
Stop leading us blackfellas around,
we want our two feet firmly on the ground.

Religion and missions have really screwed us up.
I don't know who's black and who's not,
black preachers telling us the Lord is the lot
but I know the whitefella gives cold beer when it's hot.

I know the government gives you money to sit down.
Why work when you can go drinking around
but there's only one thing I'd like to see
is stopping black deaths in custody.

Today I see a tribe who's uneasy and sad
the do-gooders don't know it but they're driving us mad.
Education is a must for today,
our tribal customs must always stay.

It's dog eat dog in this world today,
killer instinct we must develop and make it stay.
Challenge problems, not running away,
forget about the booze and family fights,
let's stand up as individuals and make it right.

So back off and give me some space,
it's gunna be me running this race.
So please leave us alone
I'd like to be left on my own.

Elders

Look
at the elders
as they
talk
with their hands.

They are
like trees
in
our beautiful land.

Listen
to the elders
as they tell
of
long time ago.

Watch
the elders
as they
take aim
with their spear.

For they
are like
the Kimberley rains
so far
yet so near.

Let's

The children
are men and women
of tomorrow.
Let's look after
mother earth
so they won't be
burdened with sorrow.

Let the trees
reach for the heavens.
Let the sand
move with the tide.
Let the
children have fun.
Let's protect the ozone layer
so our children
won't have to hide
from the midday sun.

New beginning

Sliding
down rainbows,
chasing moonbeams,
tranquillity and serenity,
life is so happy
it seems.

Cool rain
cascading
on parched land,
blustery winds,
the moving sands.

Life is wonderful,
we can understand
smiling faces.
Life is not over,
new beginning
because—we're sober.

Calling Thought

Michael J. Smith

In the year 2000, I have been around the sun thirty-six times. Born in Perth. Lived on Northam Reserve for three years with my family. Most of my school years were at Greenmount Primary, first and second year at Foothills High in Guildford and then Governor Stirling Senior High in West Midland. Started work as an apprentice chef. I lived with my foster mother until I was old enough to leave home. At the age of nineteen, I lived and studied at Tranby College in Sydney. Turning twenty-two, I moved to Broome to meet my father and his family. I also met my family at Warmun (Turkey Creek), Kija people. This move started my journey of healing and then came my poetry writing. I do say thank you to Aboriginality. Peace, love and understanding to those who read my work.

My introduction to healthwork came when I moved to Broome, with the Kimberley Aboriginal Medical Service Council (KAMSC), and also Broome Regional Aboriginal Medical Service (BRAMS). I worked with the Perth Aboriginal Medical Centre, and Danila Dilbah Aboriginal Counselling Service in Darwin. Acting for videos and plays about health issues was part of my role. I was a cast member in the musical *Corrugation Road* by Jimmy Chi. I am now living in Armidale NSW, studying the Bachelor of Counselling program at the University of New England.

Photo courtesy of KAMSC.

Contents

Dedicated to the healing of the stolen generations. To all my grandmothers, for the wisdom and love they teach. To my mother, for giving me life and being who you are, thank you. To Mrs Bender, my foster mother, for the love and respect in life's skills that makes me who I am today. To the importance of family, and to those who are close to me, you know who you are. To my very dear friend Sue Laird, who has taught me the stability of self.

Butterflies dance

Butterflies come to the water
from mountains, valleys, hills and plains.
Why is it that they come to kiss the salt of the ocean?
Dancing above the waves I see them, there, there,
the butterfly is gone
in the motion of the ocean
or maybe in the belly of a fish.
Your colours belong to you
I shall not speak of their beauty
Butterfly, butterfly dance the dance to die
come kiss the salt of the ocean.

Movement

Move into light when darkness
is behind you
for you will enter into
the realm of knowingness.
Until you have this realisation
your thoughts are not purely yours
but are of many others that are a part
of your earthly presence.
Justify.

Where

I've really only ever known you once
long time ago though can't remember you clearly,
I was looking through naive lies.
Forgetting you, don't know where you are,
haven't found you since then.
Where does one look for something
as precious as you?
Searched and searched
my time and time for you,
haven't found you after all these years.
Gotta be careful that I don't stop looking for you though,
love,
'cos wouldn't that be lonely?

Kija calling

Walk they did
how far I can't tell.
Here to there, they say,
but not with kilometres in mind,
it's not important to the experience.
Nanna she walked too, with her sister—
same story those two did tell, but at different times
for now Nanna is gone.
Family from Argyle
long time we never knew you,
years of growing we heard about you
now finally we meet—
how proud the gift.
The eldest sister the gardiya did steal,
two and one brother left behind you see.
There is a cave Nanna did visit with her family
put her handprint, her grandfather did,
to show this is country
to her bloodline.
Aboriginality thank you,
so intimate the feeling.

The bleeding moon

Sahul Sahul from you I see the moon's full glow.
You've seen the red moon like time itself
Gondwana.
Half the night it glows to the west
not many stars I sight in this half of the night.
In the east of the sky, it's dark
with stars so bright.
There is a line in the sky tonight that makes it
bright to the darkest light.
Sunglasses I wear in the brightest half of this night,
the eclipse of the moon I sight tonight.
Sahul you've seen this night
even before man had sight I suppose,
Sahul Sahul so mystic is the eclipse
of the bleeding moon.

Red tears brown pain

Hello old one
how is your monumental physique these days?
A scar you have on your fixed stature
too many travel to sweat-walk your back, old one.
They never heard the sacred cries,
only your guardians weep the tears
to endure the pain.
Uluru, tears and pain
old one.
In time the welter of our tears
will heal the scars
Indigenous Australia carries.

Over the sea

Come dance with me Eastern lover
cover me with your body scents
it's your honey-licked skin that stings my eyes
like a wasp would its victim.
The pain so majestic, of your beauty
let our bodies caress with intertwining motion
let our spirits come to enjoy the splendour
come dance with me Eastern lover.

Sha la la

Sha la la for indecisiveness
let us not show haste to impatience
for people change the ideals of their minds
so let's not judge
for we are guilty to indecisiveness.
Remember that our minds
are our tools to change.
There, let our thoughts click in
and out of our reality of decision-making.
It is me and you, be patient
for understanding can be probable.
Find it and show no more haste to impatience
Sha la la.

Calling thought

The calling in mot juste is yours
but listen to those of ancient time
for they are the knowing ones.
Some of us have the gift—
for those who do, listen listen listen
Those hearing move to remember what was said
in the silence of time
for time unfolds many ancient gifts
if we care to grasp them
inside thoughts.

Potential lover

You turn me
I hear myself think
Did I plan this? Your presence in my time
or is it yourself I seek?
To look at you I feel torment of mind
that I justify with inside motion,
such as you is great to meet, a friend
when a friend is needed
pleasurable patience I have for you,
you are near but yet so far at times
but this, in you, I like.
Trust and honesty of mine is yours
but not love, for love is hard to find
and when you have it, it's hard to forget.
You have such a way about you
that I cannot explain
to expose this would be shattering
for your unexplainable self is what I like most about you
love, lovely, lover......

Reserve reserve

Up and down along the river we ran
on the first path past a place called Island Farm
we would look towards town
coming closer and closer as we ran.
A second path led down to the river
where fishes that once swam would poison you
if they were to pierce your skin,
gilgies are hidden inside.
A snake that is sacred lives there too.
He is a part of me
and you who come from the valley.
New blue tin were the houses built then
in town too, the houses were tin.
One ditch was there
one swing as well
that bloody bobtail he knew one hall, one TV and all,
we would sit and stare at that place near the wall.
Childhood memories are happiest
never sad or cold on the reserve we called home
only warmth and happiness left, that's all.
Remembering the old ones is a great gift you know
reserve, reserve, you were my home.

Belonging

Is it a feeling?
We know not of where it comes.
Does this grow with us as we are forming
in the wombs of our mothers,
or is it what we learn as we see the experience
of day to night and night to day.
Within earth's essence we exist with belonging
as well do space and time—
not knowing belonging is where you and me endure
suffering.

Cold cement

I heard him say,
'I can't fly,'
as he remembers
the cold dark bars
that his thoughts can see beyond,
as he describes an eagle
without wings.

He says it's the white man's depravation
that they have squelched into our being
Prison memories.

Roller-roller

We would run, you would spin
you were loud with noise, we would laugh with joy.
You were dented, we were proud if you had more.
Of a milk tin you were born
dust was created as you would spin and roll
inside of you was packed with sand and stone.
We would run and run to help you win,
amused looks on my face when I remember you now
roller-roller, you were my playmate, my friend.

Day today

What's that day?
It's not Monday
or Tuesday,
is it the day after that?
Don't know, is it tomorrow day?
Oh well, too many days to think about
I'll just sit here and think about today day.

Suffering

Walking along the world before me
I have a stirring inside that I have known many times before
feelings belonging to this country
that my forefathers have known.
If only I could hear them singing
the feeling would be overwhelming
that my soul would shun their screams and cries
that their world has endured.

War dump

Twisting, sharp dark crevices
moulded together above the shoreline
The beauty beyond the water level is charismatic of its origins.
The sharp dark crevices are not of its own,
but of those who came there.
To look into this place you are to see the horror,
frightened ones who just don't know
energy lost
subsiding memories.

Skin

Flakes of us are minute
deadlings which fall from you
but knowing not of where they fall.
This motion surely must be existence, existing.
We exist to always flake deadlings.
To keep our skin
moist in motion of life
is to be human.

I

Where am I to go? I ask.
I don't know, I answer.
Will this turn in life be what I'm looking for
or will I be in passing in others lives?
I don't know, I answer.
Do I want in life what I think
or do I want what others would like to see?
I don't know, I answer.
Just remember, I am here—
not where I was—
Look at me.

Heducation

'What it tis, that place where them
young wadjula kids go?'
'Don't know,' one said to the other
as the two old dark-skinned people sat and gossiped.
'Must ask the boss man.'
The first one thought this thought over
frightened of a neglected answer,
the question took time to present itself,
just like the one who asked.

The boss man looked
as a trickle of sweat ran to the side of his radish face
from its position above his brow.
His answer was swift but blunt,
'Don't you people know anything?
It's school, it's where our children go
so they can have a better future
and a successful job.'
The old ones thoughts were baffling.
We got good job on this farm
but what's this word heducation,
them wadjula fellas they got funny meaning!
Must be we and our children can find this heducation.

Heducation they had not,
them mob from yesteryear.
Education we have today
be proud to obtain it
and be sure to use it with success
for education will lead our people into the future.
Education is knowledge
and knowledge can be power.

Cradle education with a balanced objective
and we the dark-skinned people will succeed—
Henceforth, educate our babies,
for they are and will be our future.

Nullarbor Crossing
1970

One road—before tar
I knew it
One car four people
we knew it
One black man with dust and boomerang
he knew it
We stopped and talked, big mobs appeared
they knew it
One woman she saw me I saw her
She shouted 'Hey, little black one'
we knew it
This road covered in dust, us too
along with them
it knew it
The Nullarbor Plain
do you know it?
'Cos others passing with a courteous wave
they knew it
this road full of dust—before tar

Wine along

Long time I bin doin' this—
gotta start lookin' at the world proper
hard though, when I have no wine along.
I shake and shout
even a little frighten
need some more wine along
to stop this feeling so strange.
Forgotten how, how to be myself
just don't know me anymore
wine along no good in our life
make us fight make us jealous too.
Gotta get the drink away from me
that drinking no good
wine along you the devil I can see
you the bastard
that makes life hell.

Planetation

Why do we turn? said someone's thought.
If we stop to turn will we fall?
Not knowing a true answer,
we will never be rid of this thought.
Will we fall off this planet into space,
or does the world slip on its axis,
to form a new time that we will never know—
world over.

The end

Jenny doesn't like the world today
she says it's scorched
becoming slightly burnt.
So one great voice had said to our predecessors—
how does one of so long ago
see through decades of time,
does this voice see it as a mirror image
or does this voice understand human existence?
Maybe we will never know until another
great voice says
'The end.'

Escape

To look is what we perceive,
without knowing is our prejudice,
why does life turn in such a manner,
will we fully understand our human being
or is our beingness like a wave of a hand
to forget wrongfulness?
Let's not dwell in the past tense,
to look at the world from afar.
Would we know it as it turns
profusely,
why is life not so
understanding,
knowing would not matter
therefore prejudice would have no existence.
Escape from prejudice.

Spiritual calling

We are not of your world,
we come from a dark passage
beyond your thoughts.
It is balanced, quiet, and full of worldly wisdom,
the place of where we come.
It could be yours
if you care to find us within your mature minds
within your global sphere
there are no more than just a few,
spread far
and wide are you.
Messages are unforseeing
hear them first then unfold them into other minds,
as you walk and talk to those who
are searching for meaning to their being.
For this would be special
to your next turn of outer body existence.
As many travellers have done so in the past,
more will endeavour to do so within the future.
As we strive to be a part of your earthly presence,
within spirituality, guidance is apparent
to this your place in time.
Excel informantly to those with
spiritual minds.

Identity

Identity
what is this word,
it's not of my cousins,
it comes from the white-skinned
who stole it from our being
as they became more and more in our land—
to do such a thing is not nice.
For some time this has happened,
this identity
scorned out of our truth.
Aboriginal we are
and Aboriginal we will stay.
For we know who we are
even though
it is through torment of mind.
For us urbanised blacks
we have a new way of life,
so does this mean we have a new
concrete and tar Culture?
As far as the eye can see we don't have spears
kangaroo fur across our bodies,
no more stone axes,
even the mia mia has gone from our lives.
Remembering that the old ways have turned
to the new ways,
this new identity is who we are today.
Agree to Disagree.

1996 Massacre in Van Diemen's Land

Yes, I still hear my kin from the southern land
I hear your screams, I hear your cries
gun shots echo with your history.
I've even heard the reason why.
Remember, remember, how your being became
in Van Diemen's Land
whiteman.
Thirty-five of yours massacred today—
tribal people wiped out,
you know.
Screams,
blood,
death,
tears,
confusion,
faces of horror.
Do you feel the pain like I do?
Can you understand why, I don't!
Massacre in Van Diemen's Land,
you have become a massacrer once more,
look now through my heart and eyes,
feel and see what I do, whiteman.
Massacre in Van Diemen's Land—
it's you who have done it twice.

Ancestral history: 40,000 years along

Forty thousand years you
my people
have lived
a serene existence
with your
harmonious surroundings,
who die
then enter into the earth
and become once more.
Just like you my ancestor,
whose history has changed
with slight movement.
Colonisation has made
a quick impact to change.
Must find meaning to this life,
so many bad things
we hear of the past.
Gunshots, death, screams of rape,
mournful cries of those
whose children were snatched.
Some of us still hear them
distant colonial voices
saying that our culture is heathenous,
but to what avail are these words spoken?
We are people of today and tomorrow.
To have radios, cars,
houses, clothes, money,
and other material things in our lives,
do we forget our ancestral being?
Let us say not,
for some of us are
contemporary Aborigines
who live in this society of change.

Ancestors of tomorrow will look
back on another forty thousand years
they too will have change.
Ancestral plain to change.

Ha Ha

Wesley wakes,
not knowing
if time in thought would suffice
with existence today.
A minute in time is not known until you are in it,
one minute behind you is time
is undoable.
His thoughts are of his own
like each one's are,
ha ha time just went
but thoughts under the consciousness
are not known,
remain just, in time,
unknown.

'riginie

'riginie you deadly you know
eh, you remember him, that one
you know that one that come here
long time ago
and made us half.
But you know what,
we more deadly because we know
how to live in that fella's world—
two we got now.
Mustn't forget to teach the young ones the old ways,
cause that fella he bin force us to live his way,
not fair eh.
'riginie don't stay sad
because them mob they starting to remember us
and when they all know us
it'll be fucken more and more solid
Eh 'riginie we must become one voice
that them mob from faraway longtime can understand
but 'riginie, remember our own countries,
we stay proper strong in our spirit.
Eh 'riginie, you deadly you know.

Pauline

Your face structure is like that
of a twit giving birth to its young.
please, tell us YOUR history,
for I see that you are not many generations into this country
as I am.
People of your race are true barbarians
you come, you take over,
then you have the cheek to complain about others
who would like to live here too.
You can have your say
but let us not heed your praise
for I see you are a jester.
You are the idiot in the harlequin colours
When will you let the stench of the deepfryer caress your
person and disappear back from where you once henced
with your *knowledge* that is not applicable to this
our multicultural country.

Armidale Jack

Jack is to watch and tell,
A tale of him I'll try and tell
I see him daily in the freshest light
Just like him, so short and staunch, I see his tail
Of himself he can't speak,
for he is of K9 heritage
Barks and barks if he is unfamiliar with your smell,
He walks his realm he does,
so engrained is the path he walks
with a military flair
Then he rests on grass under the sun
to warm his aging bones
there, I've told my tale,
of my new friend Armidale Jack.

Just never knew

You look la me, I look la you,
what do we la two see, in la one
and one too la two, la you,
la me we two la see.
Yuwayi, yuwayi, it's we who blung
la Kimberley
but more talk la dis way,
you fella know.
It blung you fella from bush.
Bush blung Granny, you fella,
Kija granny did blung.
La language, two she did speak.
Ay poor fella, poor fella don't know much
my language
so I just write this creole.